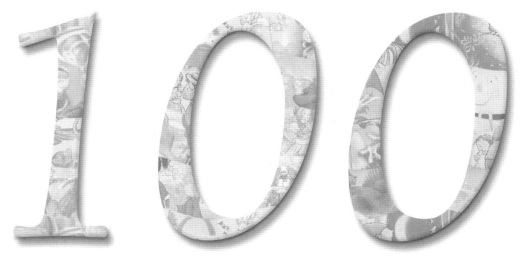

100
BEST-LOVED
NURSERY RHYMES

First published in 2002 by Miles Kelly Publishing Ltd,
The Bardfield Centre, Great Bardfield, Essex, CM7 4SL

Copyright © Miles Kelly Publishing Ltd 2002

This edition printed in 2008

8 10 12 14 15 13 11 9

Project Editors: Belinda Gallagher, Isla MacCuish
Designers: Michelle Cannatella, Debbie Meekcoms
Cover Design: Debbie Meekcoms
Reprints Controller: Bethan Ellish
Production Manager: Elizabeth Brunwin
Reprographics: Anthony Cambray

ISBN 978-1-84236-123-8

Printed in China

British Library Cataloguing-in-Publication Data
A catalogue record for this book is available from the British Library

Cover artwork by Priscilla Lamont

All other images from the Miles Kelly Archives

www.mileskelly.net
info@mileskelly.net

www.factsforprojects.com

BEST-LOVED
NURSERY RHYMES

Contents

Play Together Rhymes

Animal Rhymes

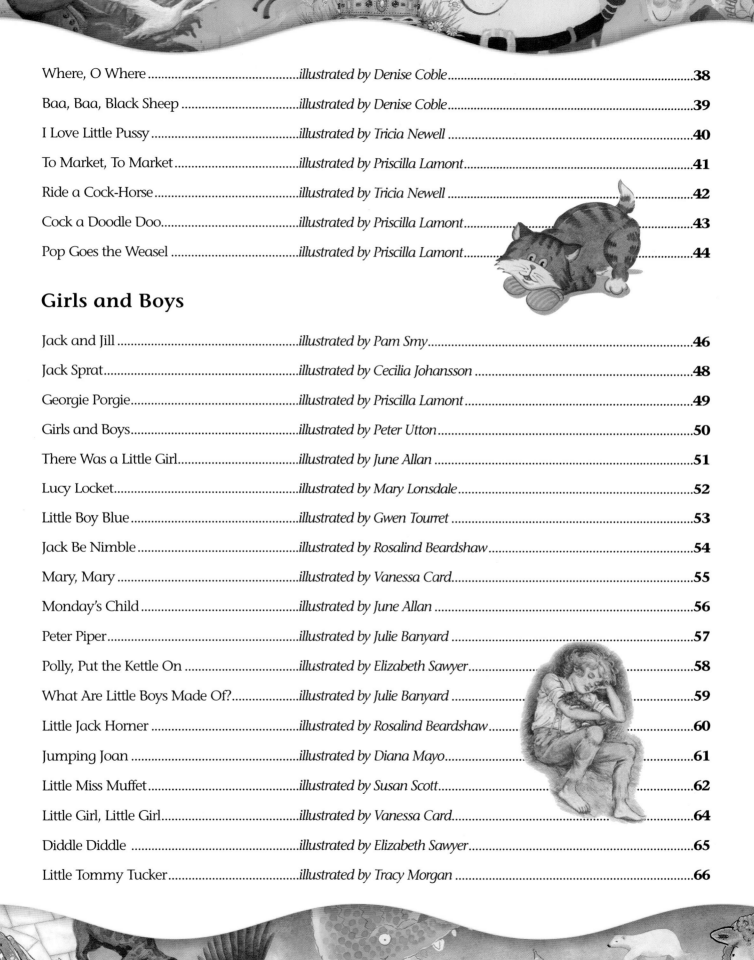

Girls and Boys

Number Rhymes

Favourite Folk

Best-Loved Rhymes

Bedtime Rhymes

Play Together Rhymes

Round and Round the Garden

Round and round the garden

Like a teddy bear;

One step, two step,

Tickle you under there!

Draw circles with your finger around the palm.

Walk your fingers up the arm in two steps.

Tickle under the arm!

Here Is the Church

Here is the church, and here is the steeple;

Open the door and here are the people.

Here is the parson going upstairs,

And here he is a-saying his prayers.

Put palms together and link fingers downwards to form the church. Point index fingers up to form the spire. Turn hands over and wiggle the fingers to be the people.

11

This Little Pig

This little pig
went to market,
This little pig stayed at home,
This little pig had roast beef,
This little pig had none,
And this little pig cried,
'Wee-wee-wee-wee-wee,'
All the way home.

Read the first line and wiggle the big toe.

Read the next line and wiggle the next toe and so on...

On the final line tickle the foot.

Play Together

Pat-a-Cake

Pat-a-cake, pat-a-cake, baker's man,

Bake me a cake as fast as you can;

Roll it and pat it and mark it with 'B',

And put it in the oven for baby

and me.

Clap your hands together then pat the palms of your partner. Repeat this action as you sing the rhyme.

Oranges and Lemons

Oranges and Lemons,

Say the bells of St. Clement's.

You owe me five farthings,

Say the bells of St. Martin's.

When will you pay me?

Say the bells of Old Bailey.

When I grow rich,

Say the bells of Shoreditch.

Two children representing oranges and lemons form an arch. The other children pass beneath. On the final verse, the arch falls and the child beneath chooses to stand behind 'oranges' or 'lemons'.

Play Together

When will that be?

Say the bells of Stepney.

I do not know,

Says the great bell of Bow.

Here comes a candle

To light you to bed.

Here comes a chopper

To chop off your head!

Ring-a-Ring o' Roses

Ring-a-ring o' roses,

A pocket full of posies,

A-tishoo! A-tishoo!

We all fall down.

All hold hands and skip round in a ring. On the last line of each verse all sit down on the ground.

16

See-Saw, Margery Daw

See-saw, Margery Daw,

Johnny shall have a new master;

He shall have but a penny a day,

Because he can't work any faster.

An ideal rhyme for playing in the park. Or sit on the floor facing your partner holding hands. Gently rock backwards and forwards as if you were on a see-saw.

Play Together

Two Little Dickie-Birds

Two little dickie-birds,

Sitting on a wall,

One named Peter,

The other named Paul;

Fly away, Peter!

Fly away, Paul!

Come back, Peter!

Come back, Paul!

Use your index fingers to be Peter and Paul. Wiggle each finger in turn. Next, put each finger behind you as if to fly away. On the last line, bring each finger back in front of you.

18

Play Together

I'm a Little Teapot

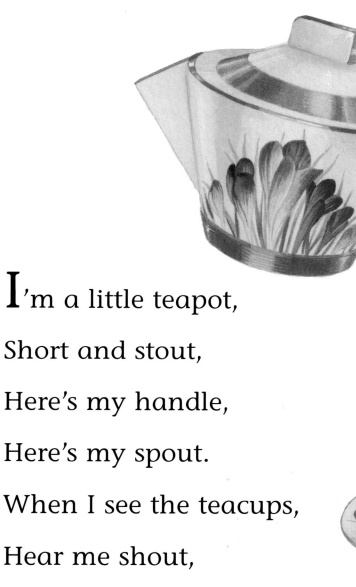

I'm a little teapot,

Short and stout,

Here's my handle,

Here's my spout.

When I see the teacups,

Hear me shout,

Tip me up, and pour me out.

Place one hand on your hip to be the handle. Place the opposite arm out to the side to be the spout. On the final line, lean over to the side to pour the tea.

Play Together

The Mulberry Bush

Here we go round the mulberry bush,

The mulberry bush, the mulberry bush,

Here we go round the mulberry bush,

On a cold and frosty morning.

This is the way we wash our hands,

Wash our hands, wash our hands,

This is the way we wash our hands,

On a cold and frosty morning.

Join hands and skip round in a circle on the first verse. This is the chorus. Mime the actions in the remaining verses. After each main verse repeat the chorus.

Play Together

This is the way we wash our clothes,

Wash our clothes, wash our clothes,

This is the way we wash our clothes,

On a cold and frosty morning.

This is the way we go to school,

Go to school, go to school,

This is the way we go to school,

On a cold and frosty morning.

This is the way we come out of school,

Come out of school, come out of school,

This is the way we come out of school,

On a cold and frosty morning.

This is the Way

This is the way the ladies ride,

Tri, tre, tre, tree, Tri, tre, tre, tree;

This is the way the ladies ride,

Tri, tre, tre, tre, tri-tre-tre-tree!

This is the way the gentlemen ride,

Gallop-a-trip, Gallop-a-trot;

This is the way the gentlemen ride,

Gallop-a-gallop-a-trot!

This is the way the farmers ride,

Hobbledy-hoy, Hobbledy-hoy;

This is the way the farmers ride,

Hobbledy, hobbledy-hoy!

*Pretend to be a lady gently
riding along.
Next pretend to be a
gentleman galloping along.
Then pretend to be the farmer
hobbling along.*

Play Together

One Potato

One potato, two potato,

Three potatoes, four,

Five potatoes, six potatoes,

Seven potatoes more.

Take turns with your partner
in placing one fist on top
of another to build a
tower. When you reach
seven start again.

23

Incy, Wincy Spider

Incy, Wincy spider

Climbed up the water spout;

Down came the rain

And washed the spider out:

Out came the sun

And dried up all the rain;

So Incy, Wincy spider

Climbed up the spout again.

Use your fingers to be the spider climbing up the spout. Wriggle your fingers to be the rain. Sweep your hands in an arch to show the sun. Use your fingers to be the spider climbing back up the spout.

Play Together

Animal Rhymes

Ding, Dong Bell

Ding, dong bell,

Pussy's in the well.

Who put her in?

Little Johnny Green.

Who pulled her out?

Little Johnny Stout.

What a naughty boy was that

To try to drown poor pussy cat,

Which never did him any harm,

But killed the mice in his father's barn.

Pussy Cat, Pussy Cat

Pussy cat, pussy cat, where
have you been?
I've been to London to look
at the queen.
Pussy cat, pussy cat, what did
you there?
I frightened a little mouse
under her chair.

Goosey, Goosey Gander

Goosey, goosey gander,

Whither shall I wander?

Upstairs and downstairs

And in my lady's chamber.

There I met an old man

Who would not say his prayers,

I took him by his left leg

And threw him down the stairs.

The Crocodile

If you should meet a crocodile

Don't take a stick and poke him.

Ignore the welcome in his smile,

Be careful not to stroke him.

For as he sleeps upon the Nile,

He thinner gets and thinner;

So whene'er you meet a crocodile

He's ready for his dinner.

Animal Rhymes

Who Killed Cock Robin?

Who killed Cock Robin?
'I,' said the sparrow,
'With my bow
and arrow,
I killed Cock Robin.'

Who saw him die?
'I,' said the fly,
'With my little eye,
I saw him die.'

Who caught his blood?
'I,' said the fish,
'With my little dish,
I caught his blood.'

Who'll dig his grave?
'I,' said the owl,
'With my spade
and trowel,
I'll dig his grave.'

Who'll be the clerk?
'I,' said the lark,
'If it's not in the dark,
I'll be the clerk.'

Who'll be the parson?
'I,' said the rook,
'With my little book,
I'll be the parson.'

Animal Rhymes

Who'll sing a psalm?

'I,' said the thrush,

As she sat on a bush,

'I'll sing a psalm.'

Who'll be chief mourner?

'I,' said the dove,

'I mourn for my love,

I'll be chief mourner.'

Who'll toll the bell?

'I,' said the bull,

'Because I can pull,

I'll toll the bell.'

All the birds of the air

Fell sighing and sobbing,

When they heard the bell toll

For poor Cock Robin.

To all it concerns,

This notice apprises,

The sparrow's for trial

At next bird assizes.

Animal Rhymes

Mary's Lamb

Mary had a little lamb,

Its fleece was white as snow;

And everywhere that Mary went

The lamb was sure to go.

Animal Rhymes

Little Bo-Peep

Little Bo-Peep has lost her sheep,

And can't tell where to find them;

Leave them alone, and they'll come home,

Bringing their tails behind them.

Animal Rhymes

The Cat and the Fiddle

Hey-diddle-diddle,

The cat and the fiddle,

The cow jumped over the moon;

The little dog laughed to see such fun,

And the dish ran away with the spoon.

34

Animal Rhymes

Hickory, Dickory, Dock

Hickory, dickory, dock,

The mouse ran up the clock.

The clock struck one,

The mouse ran down,

Hickory, dickory, dock.

Hickety, Pickety

Hickety, pickety, my fine hen,

She lays eggs for gentlemen;

Gentlemen come every day

To see what my fine hen doth lay.

Sometimes nine and somtimes ten,

Hickety, pickety, my fine hen.

Where, O Where

Where, O where,

has my little dog gone?

O where, O where, can he be?

With his tail cut short,

and his ears cut long,

O where, O where, has he gone?

Animal Rhymes

Baa, Baa, Black Sheep

Baa, baa, black sheep,

Have you any wool?

Yes, sir, yes, sir,

Three bags full;

One for my master,

One for my dame,

And one for the little boy

Who lives down the lane.

I Love Little Pussy

I love little pussy, her coat is so warm,

And if I don't hurt her, she'll do me no harm.

So I'll not pull her tail, nor drive her away,

But pussy and I very gently will play.

I'll sit by the fire, and give her some food,

And pussy will love me because I am good.

To Market, To Market

To market, to market to buy a fat pig,

Home again, home again, jiggety-jig;

To market, to market to buy a fat hog,

Home again, home again, jiggety-jog.

Animal Rhymes

Ride a Cock-Horse

Ride a cock-horse to Banbury Cross,

To see a fine lady upon a white horse;

Rings on her fingers and bells on her toes,

She shall have music wherever she goes.

Cock a Doodle Doo

Cock a doodle doo!

My dame has lost her shoe;

My master's lost his fiddling stick

And doesn't know what to do.

Pop Goes the Weasel

Up and down the City Road,

In and out of the Eagle,

That's the way the money goes,

Pop goes the weasel!

Half a pound of tuppenny rice,

Half a pound of treacle,

Mix it up and make it nice,

Pop goes the weasel!

Every night when I go out

The monkey's on the table;

Take a stick and knock it off,

Pop goes the weasel.

Girls and Boys

Jack and Jill

Jack and Jill went up the hill

To fetch a pail of water;

Jack fell down, and broke his crown,

And Jill came tumbling after.

Then up Jack got, and home did trot,

As fast as he could caper.

He went to bed,

To mend his head

With vinegar and brown paper.

47

Jack Sprat

Jack Sprat could eat no fat,

His wife could eat no lean,

So between them both, you see,

They licked the platter clean.

Jack ate all the lean,

Joan ate all the fat,

The bone they picked it clean,

Then gave it to the cat.

Georgie Porgie

Georgie Porgie, pudding and pie,

Kissed the girls and made them cry;

When the boys came out to play,

Georgie Porgie ran away.

Girls and Boys

Girls and Boys

Girls and boys, come out to play,

The moon is shining bright as day;

Leave your supper and leave your sleep,

And come with your playfellows into the street;

Come with a whoop and come with a call,

Come with a good will, or come not at all.

There Was a Little Girl

There was a little girl and she had a little curl

Right in the middle of her forehead;

When she was good, she was very, very good,

But when she was bad, she was horrid.

51

Lucy Locket

Lucy Locket lost her pocket,

Kitty Fisher found it;

There was not a penny in it,

But a ribbon round it.

Little Boy Blue

Little Boy Blue,

Come blow your horn,

The sheep's in the meadow,

The cow's in the corn.

But where is the boy

Who looks after the sheep?

He's under a haycock,

Fast asleep.

'Will you wake him?'

'No, not I,

For if I do,

He's sure to cry.'

53

Jack Be Nimble

Jack be nimble,

Jack be quick,

Jack jump over the candlestick.

Mary, Mary

Mary, Mary, quite contrary,

How does your garden grow?

With silver bells and cockle shells,

And pretty maids all in a row.

Monday's Child

Monday's child is fair of face,

Tuesday's child is full of grace,

Wednesday's child is full of woe,

Thursday's child has far to go,

Friday's child is loving and giving,

Saturday's child works hard for a living,

And the child that is born on the Sabbath day

Is bonny and blithe, and good and gay.

Girls and Boys

Peter Piper

Peter Piper picked a peck of pickled pepper;

A peck of pickled pepper Peter Piper picked.

If Peter Piper picked a peck of pickled pepper,

Where's the peck of pickled pepper

Peter Piper picked?

Polly, Put the Kettle On

Polly, put the kettle on,

Polly, put the kettle on,

Polly, put the kettle on,

And let's have tea.

Sukey, take it off again,

Sukey, take it off again,

Sukey, take it off again,

They've all gone away.

What Are Little Boys Made Of?

What are little
boys made of?
What are little
boys made of?
Frogs and snails and
puppy-dogs' tails,
That's what little boys are made of.

What are little girls made of?
What are little girls made of?
Sugar and spice
and all things nice,
That's what little girls
are made of.

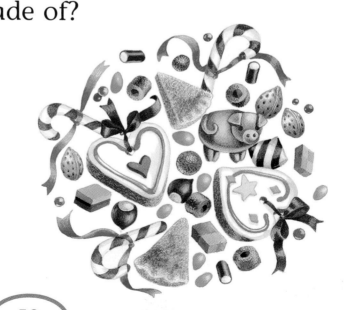

Little Jack Horner

Little Jack Horner

Sat in the corner,

Eating a Christmas pie;

He put in a thumb,

And pulled out a plum,

And said, 'What a good boy am I.'

Girls and Boys

Jumping Joan

Here I am,

Little Jumping Joan;

When nobody's with me

I'm all alone.

Little Miss Muffet

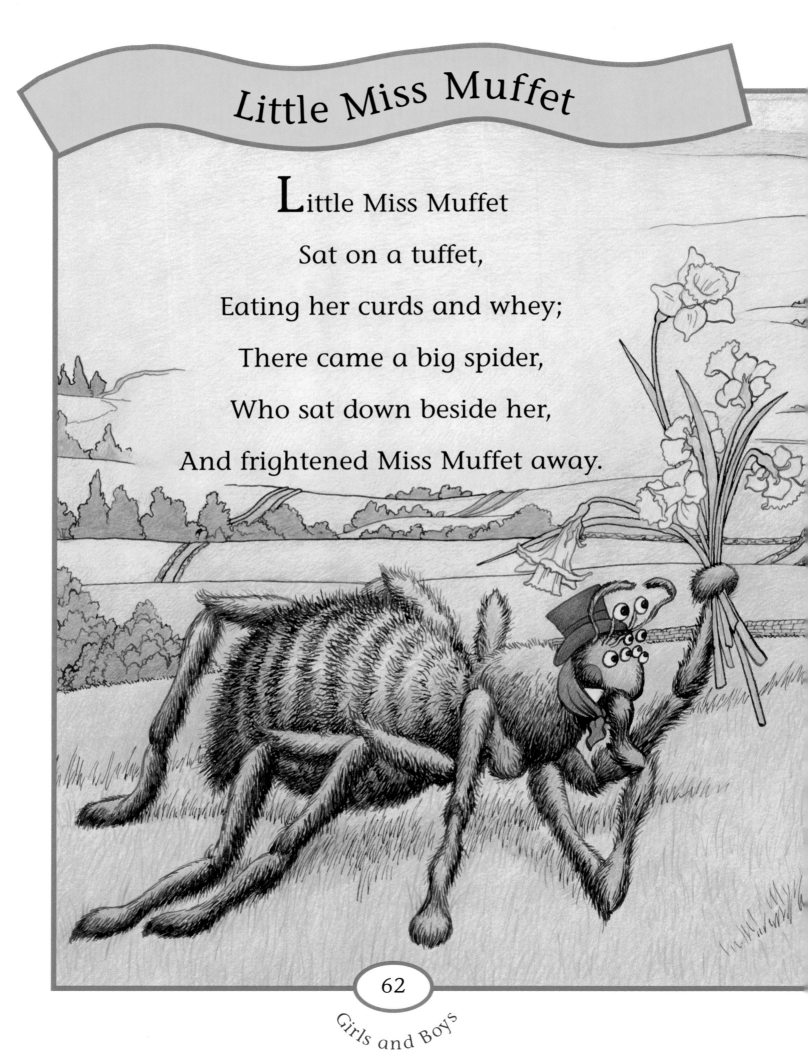

Little Miss Muffet

Sat on a tuffet,

Eating her curds and whey;

There came a big spider,

Who sat down beside her,

And frightened Miss Muffet away.

Girls and Boys

Little Girl, Little Girl

Little girl, little girl, where have you been?

Gathering roses to give to the queen.

Little girl, little girl, what gave she you?

She gave me a diamond as big as my shoe.

Diddle, Diddle, Dumpling

Diddle, diddle, dumpling, my son John,

Went to bed with his trousers on;

One shoe off, and one shoe on,

Diddle, diddle, dumpling, my son John.

Little Tommy Tucker

Little Tommy Tucker,

Sings for his supper.

What shall we give him?

White bread and butter.

How shall he cut it

Without a knife?

How will he be married

Without a wife?

66

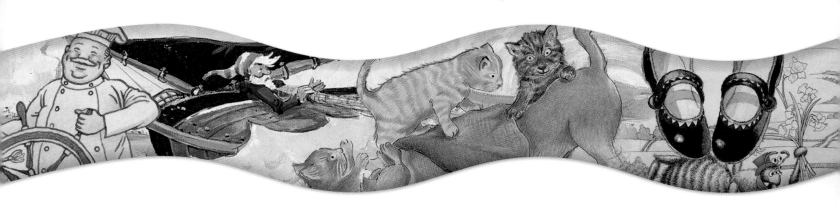

Number Rhymes

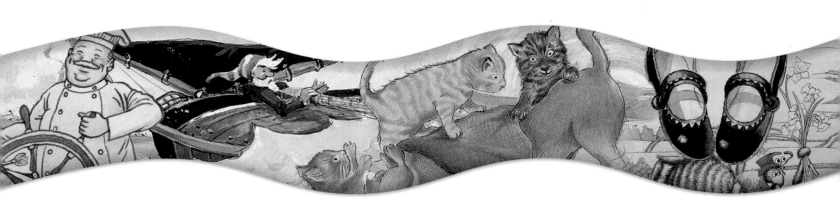

As I Was Going to St. Ives

As I was going to St. Ives,

I met a man with seven wives.

Each wife had seven sacks,

Each sack had seven cats,

Each cat had seven kits;

Kits, cats, sacks and wives,

How many were going to St. Ives?

Three Blind Mice

Three blind mice. Three blind mice.

See how they run! See how they run!

They all run after the farmer's wife,

Who cut off their tails with a carving knife.

Did you ever see such a thing in your life,

As three blind mice?

I Saw Three Ships

I saw three ships come sailing by,

Come sailing by, come sailing by,

I saw three ships come sailing by,

On New Year's Day in the morning.

And what do you think was in them then,

Was in them then, was in them then?

And what do you think was in them then,

On New Year's Day in the morning?

Three pretty girls were in them then,

Were in them then, were in them then,

Three pretty girls were in them then,

On New Year's Day in the morning.

Three Men in a Tub

Rub-a-dub-dub,

Three men in a tub;

And who do you think they be?

The butcher, the baker,

The candlestick-maker;

They all jumped out of a rotten potato,

'Twas enough to make a man stare.

I Love Sixpence

I love sixpence, pretty little sixpence,

I love sixpence better than my life;

I spent a penny of it, I spent another,

And I took fourpence home to my wife.

Oh my little fourpence, pretty little fourpence,

I love fourpence better than my life;

I spent a penny of it, I spent another,

And I took twopence home to my wife.

Oh my little twopence, pretty little twopence,

I love twopence better than my life;

I spent a penny of it, I spent another,

And I took nothing home to my wife.

Six Little Mice

Six little mice sat down to spin;

Pussy passed by and she peeped in.

'What are you doing, my little men?'

'Weaving coats for gentlemen.'

'Shall I come in and cut off your threads?'

'No, no, Mistress Pussy, you'd bite off our heads.'

'Oh, no, I'll not; I'll help you to spin.'

'That may be so, but you don't come in.'

Five Little Pussy Cats

Five little pussy cats playing near the door;

One ran and hid inside

And then there were four.

Four little pussy cats underneath a tree;

One heard a dog bark

And then there were three.

Three little pussy cats thinking what to do;

One saw a little bird

And then there were two.

Two little pussy cats sitting in the sun;

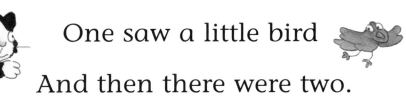

One ran to catch his tail

And then there was one.

One little pussy cat looking for some fun;

He saw a butterfly and then there was none.

Number Rhymes

One, Two, Buckle My Shoe

One, two, buckle my shoe,

Three, four, shut the door,

Five, six, pick up sticks,

Seven, eight, lay them straight,

Nine, ten, a good fat hen,

Eleven, twelve, dig and delve,

Thirteen, fourteen, maids a courting,

Fifteen, sixteen, maids in the kitchen,

Seventeen, eighteen, maids are waiting,

Nineteen, twenty, my plate's empty.

Number Rhymes

Three Little Kittens

Three little kittens, they lost their mittens,

And they began to cry,

'Oh, mother dear, we sadly fear

That we have lost our mittens.'

'What! Lost your mittens, You naughty kittens!

Then you shall have no pie.

Mee-ow, mee-ow, mee-ow.

No, you shall have no pie.'

The three little kittens, they found their mittens,

And they began to cry,

'Oh, mother dear, see here, see here,

For we have found our mittens.'

'What! Found your mittens, you silly kittens!

Then you shall have some pie.

Purr-r, purr-r, purr-r,

Oh, let us have some pie.'

One, Two, Three, Four, Five

One, two, three, four, five,

Once I caught a fish alive.

Six, seven, eight, nine, ten,

Then I let it go again.

Why did you let it go?

Because it bit my finger so.

Which finger did it bite?

This little finger on the right.

Favourite Folk

The Muffin Man

O do you know the muffin man,

The muffin man, the muffin man,

O do you know the muffin man,

That lives in Drury Lane?

O yes, I know the muffin man,

The muffin man, the muffin man,

O yes, I know the muffin man,

That lives in Drury Lane.

Favourite Folk

There Was a Crooked Man

There was a crooked man, and he went
a crooked mile,
He found a crooked
sixpence against a
crooked stile,
He bought a crooked
cat, which caught
a crooked mouse,
And they all lived
together in a little
crooked house.

Old Mother Hubbard

Old Mother Hubbard

Went to the cupboard

To get her poor dog a bone;

But when she came there

The cupboard was bare,

And so the poor dog had none.

Favourite Folk

The Queen of Hearts

The Queen of Hearts, she made some tarts,

All on a summer's day;

The Knave of Hearts, he stole the tarts,

And took them clean away.

The King of Hearts called for the tarts,

And beat the Knave full sore;

The Knave of Hearts brought back the tarts,

And vowed he'd steal no more.

Favourite Folk

Old King Cole

Old King Cole was a merry old soul,

And a merry old soul was he;

He called for his pipe, and he called

for his bowl,

And he called for his fiddlers three.

Every fiddler, he had a fine fiddle,

And a very fine fiddle had he;

Oh, there's none so rare as can compare

With King Cole and his fiddlers three.

Favourite Folk

Bobby Shaftoe

Bobby Shaftoe's
gone to sea,
Silver buckles
on his knee;
He'll come back
and marry me,
Bonny Bobby Shaftoe!

Bobby Shaftoe's young and fair,
Combing down his yellow hair;
He's my love for evermore,
Bonny Bobby Shaftoe!

Favourite Folk

The Old Woman Who Lived in a Shoe

There was an old woman

who lived in a shoe,

She had so many children

she didn't know what to do.

She gave them some broth

without any bread;

She whipped them all soundly

and put them to bed.

Favourite Folk

Favourite Folk

Humpty Dumpty

Humpty Dumpty sat on a wall,

Humpty Dumpty had a great fall;

All the king's horses and

all the king's men

Couldn't put Humpty together again.

Favourite Folk

Favourite Folk

It's Raining

It's raining, it's pouring,

The old man is snoring,

He went to bed and bumped his head,

And couldn't get up in the morning.

Simple Simon

Simple Simon met a pieman,

Going to the fair;

Says Simple Simon to the pieman,

'Let me taste your ware.'

Says the pieman to Simple Simon,

'Show me first your penny.'

Says Simple Simon to the pieman,

'Indeed I have not any.'

There Was an Old Woman

There was an old woman tossed

up in a basket,

Seventeen times as high as the moon;

And where she was going I couldn't but ask it,

For in her hand she carried a broom.

'Old woman, old woman, old woman,' said I,

'O whither, O whither, O whither so high?'

'To sweep the cobwebs off the sky!

And I'll be with you by and by.'

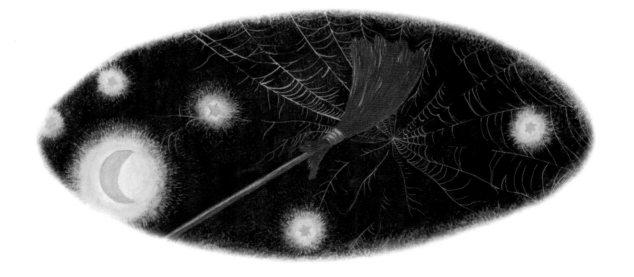

Favourite Folk

Curly Locks

Curly Locks, Curly Locks,

Wilt thou be mine?

Thou shalt not wash dishes,

Nor yet feed the swine;

But sit on a cushion,

And sew a fine seam,

And feed upon strawberries,

Sugar and cream.

Doctor Foster

Doctor Foster went to Gloucester

In a shower of rain;

He stepped in a puddle,

Right up to his middle,

And never went there again.

Yankee Doodle

Yankee Doodle came to town,

Riding on a pony;

He stuck a feather in his cap

And called it macaroni.

Yankee doodle, doodle do,

Yankee doodle dandy,

All the lasses are so smart,

And sweet as sugar candy.

Duke of York

Oh the grand old Duke of York,

He had ten thousand men;

He marched them up to the top of the hill,

And he marched them down again.

And when they were up they were up,

And when they were down they were down.

And when they were only half-way up,

They were neither up nor down.

Favourite Folk

Best-Loved Rhymes

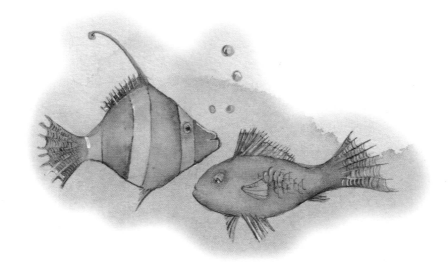

Rain, Rain

Rain, rain, go away,

Come again another day;

Little Tommy wants to play.

As I Was Going Out

As I was going out one day
My head fell off and rolled away.
But when I saw that it was gone,
I picked it up and put it on.

And when I got into the street
A fellow cried, 'Look at your feet!'
I looked at them and sadly said,
'I've left both asleep in bed!'

Hot-Cross Buns

Hot-cross Buns!

Hot-cross Buns!

One a penny, two a penny,

Hot-cross Buns!

Hot-cross Buns!

Hot-cross Buns!

If you have no daughters

Give them to your sons.

I Had a Little Nut Tree

I had a little nut tree, nothing would it bear

But a silver nutmeg and a golden pear;

The King of Spain's daughter came to visit me;

And all was because of my little nut tree.

I skipped over water, I danced over sea,

And all the birds in the air couldn't catch me.

Lavender's Blue

Lavender's blue, dilly, dilly,

Lavender's green;

When I am king, dilly, dilly,

You shall be queen.

Who told you so, dilly, dilly,

Who told you so?

'Twas mine own heart, dilly, dilly,

That told me so.

Call up your men, dilly, dilly,

Set them to work,

Some to the plough, dilly, dilly,

Some to the fork.

Some to make hay, dilly, dilly,

Some to reap corn,

Whilst you and I, dilly, dilly

Keep ourselves warm.

Roses are red, dilly, dilly,

Violets are blue;

Because you love me, dilly, dilly,

I will love you.

Best-Loved Rhymes

Sing a Song of Sixpence

Sing a song of sixpence,

A pocket full of rye;

Four and twenty blackbirds,

Baked in a pie.

When the pie was opened,

The birds began to sing;

Was not that a dainty dish,

To set before the king?

The king was in his counting-house,

Counting out his money;

The queen was in the parlour,

Eating bread and honey.

The maid was in the garden,

Hanging out the clothes,

When down came a blackbird,

And pecked off her nose.

Best-Loved Rhymes

The North Wind Doth Blow

The north wind doth blow,

And we shall have snow,

And what will poor robin do then,

poor thing?

He'll sit in a barn,

And keep himself warm,

And hide his head under his wing,

poor thing.

Christmas Is Coming

Christmas is coming,

the geese are getting fat;

Please to put a penny in the old man's hat;

If you haven't got a penny,

ha'penny will do.

If you haven't got a

ha'penny, God bless you.

If All the Seas Were One Sea

If all the seas were one sea,

What a great sea that would be!

If all the trees were one tree,

What a great tree that would be!

If all the axes were one axe,

What a great axe that would be!

And if all the men were one man,

What a great man that would be!

And if the great man took the great axe

And cut down the great tree

And let it fall into the great sea,

What a splish-splash that would be!

Dance to Your Daddie

Dance to your daddie,

My bonnie laddie,

Dance to your daddie, my bonnie lamb;

You shall get a fishie,

On a little dishie,

You shall get a herring when the boat comes home.

Dance to your daddie,

My bonnie laddie,

Dance to your daddie, and to your mammie sing;

You shall get a coatie;

And a pair of breekies,

You shall get a coatie when the boat comes in.

Red Sky at Night

Red sky at night,

Shepherd's delight;

Red sky in the morning,

Shepherd's warning.

O Dear, What Can the Matter Be?

O dear, what can the matter be?

Dear, dear, what can the matter be?

O dear, what can the matter be?

Johnny's so long at the fair.

He promised to bring me a basket of posies,

A garland of lilies, a garland of roses,

A little straw hat, to set off the ribbons

That tie up my bonny brown hair.

Row, Row

Row, row, row your boat,

Gently down the stream.

Merrily, merrily, merrily, merrily,

Life is but a dream.

Pease Pudding

Pease pudding hot,

Pease pudding cold,

Pease pudding in the pot,

Nine days old.

Some like it hot,

Some like it cold,

Some like it in the pot,

Nine days old.

Over the Hills

Tom, he was a
piper's son,
He learned to
play when he
was young,
And all the tune
that he could play
Was 'over the hills
and a great
way off,
The wind shall
blow my top
knot off'.

Blow, Wind, Blow

Blow, wind, blow, and go, mill, go,

That the miller may grind his corn;

That the baker may take it,

And into bread make it,

And bring us a loaf in the morn.

London Bridge is Falling Down

London Bridge is falling down,

Falling down, falling down,

London Bridge is falling down,

My fair lady.

Best-Loved Rhymes

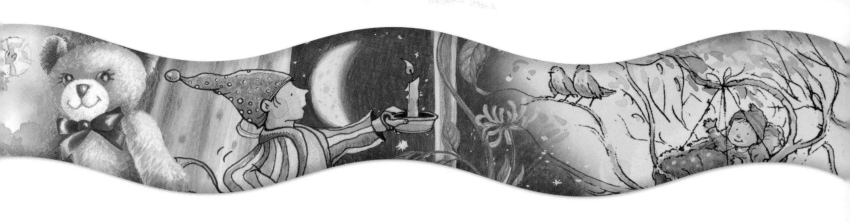

Bedtime Rhymes

Rock-a-Bye Baby

Rock-a-bye baby,

On the tree top.

When the wind blows

The cradle will rock;

When the bough breaks

The cradle will fall.

Down will come baby,

Cradle and all.

Bedtime Rhymes

Twinkle, Twinkle, Little Star

Twinkle, twinkle, little star,

How I wonder what you are.

Up above the world so high,

Like a diamond in the sky.

Come, Let's To Bed

Come, let's to bed, says Sleepy-head;

Sit up awhile, says Slow;

Bang on the pot, says Greedy-gut,

We'll sup before we go.

To bed, to bed, cried Sleepy-head,

But all the rest said No!

It is morning now,

You must milk the cow,

And tomorrow to bed we go.

Hush, Little Baby

Hush, little baby, don't say a word,

Papa's going to buy you a mocking bird.

If the mocking bird won't sing,

Papa's going to buy you a diamond ring.

If the diamond ring turns to brass,

Papa's going to buy you a looking-glass.

If the looking-glass get broke,

Papa's going to buy you a billy-goat.

If that billy-goat runs away,

Papa's going to buy you another today.

Bedtime Rhymes

Sleep, Baby, Sleep

Sleep, baby, sleep,

Thy father guards the sheep;

Thy mother shakes the dreamland tree

And from it fall sweet dreams for thee,

Sleep, baby, sleep.

Sleep, baby, sleep,

Our cottage vale is deep;

The little lamb is on the green,

The woolly fleece so soft and clean

Sleep, baby, sleep.

Sleep, baby, sleep,

Down where the woodbines creep;

Be always like the lamb so mild,

A kind and sweet and gentle child,

Sleep, baby, sleep.

Bye Baby Bunting

Bye baby bunting,

Father's gone a hunting,

To get a little rabbit-skin,

To wrap his little baby in.

Wee Willie Winkie

Wee Willie Winkie runs through the town,

Upstairs and downstairs in his nightgown,

Rapping at the window,

crying through the lock,

'Are the children in their beds,

for it's now eight o'clock?'

126

Star Light, Star Bright

Star light, star bright,

First star I see tonight,

I wish I may, I wish I might,

Have the wish I wish tonight.

I See the Moon

I see the moon,

And the moon sees me;

God bless the moon,

And God bless me.